STATES OF EMERGENCY

States
of
Emergency

YOYO COMAY

THE POETRY IMPRINT AT VÉHICULE PRESS

Published with the generous assistance of the Canada Council for the Arts and the Canada Book Fund of the Department of Canadian Heritage.

 Canada Council Conseil des arts
for the Arts du Canada

SIGNAL EDITIONS EDITOR: CARMINE STARNINO

Cover design by David Drummond
Photograph of author by Kirk Lisajp
Set in Minion and Filosofia by Simon Garamond
Printed by Livres Rapido Books

Dépôt légal, Library and Archives Canada and the Bibliothèque national du Québec, third trimester 2023

Library and Archives Canada Cataloguing in Publication

Title: States of emergency / Yoyo Comay.
Names: Comay, Yoyo, author.
Identifiers: Canadiana (print) 2023051815x | Canadiana (ebook) 20230518192 | ISBN 9781550656374 (softcover) | ISBN 9781550656459 (EPUB)
Subjects: LCGFT: Poetry.
Classification: LCC PS8605.O495 S73 2023 | DDC C811/.6—dc23

Published by Véhicule Press, Montréal, Québec, Canada
www.vehiculepress.com

Distribution in Canada by LitDistCo
www.litdistco.ca

Printed in Canada on FSC certified paper.

For Hélène

CONTENTS

ONE

I inhale history and fate:
that hollow scream
upon which
we all are strung up

life is in the foisting, the dis-
ease we pass on, pass off
for hope, pass over

I write here to aerate,
to exhume some crick or impulse
and allow it the brief bloom
of its undoing, to ease
the embolism

words are embellishment,
run off, dirt figures,
effluence, symptom

we symptom up the air
with our speaking.
we were once gutted, lodged
between liver and other viscera

now I sound to ravel,
to encartilage air,
the ribs of the throat
laying a palm
upon the earwhorl

this scream earthworms
through time, displacing
sediment—rounded shreds
of clay encompass
the aperture

language becomes organized,
swollen, inflamed

the indigestible seed,
the molar-cracking pit,
which we pass back and forth
along the canal of our breathing

this empty column
upon which we are hilted,
propped like stuffed dolls

gut-ridden inde–
cision

(to absorb and excrete
the sweat suggests
a certain stress level)

a secret roiling
deposits the slickness
of its uncertainty
on the skins bared surfaces

perhaps this upset is all
the language under lock
in the body's black abscesses

life's appendices,
low-hanging stars
set to blow
at any moment

the body's flickering fruit,
sordid ripeness
of the extremities,
the mouth organ,
its reedy calloused blow
honking on about the news

while a morsel of lunch
sups on a tucked-away patch
of untouched enamel,
filching a last sweet sadness
from the dying day

filch filch filch filch

all this suddenness
mounts up and
disgorges

to allow for the slickness of
Now

—to surf the surfeit
and emerge in excess

to bloom not blush not blanch
in this most extremest of wakes

in the skull's catafalques
the wrecked ships left rotting

let this death enliven
us, let it wrest us
from habit's soft harms

charm the day into subsistence,
crawl fruits from its rough clutches

my body is a restless patch of sundry

I want the light
to capsize me
into belieflessness
and allow me nothing
but blinks

pouring suffering like concrete
into molds, monuments
and then watch
as they succumb
to the comings
and goings
of snow,
sucked in

then out
of their grey porous flesh

the mutations of sight—
all I can see is the buzzing
fluid forming whole
globules of colour
into material reality

the momentum of this flashing,
its mounting pressure
displeasures me into
an arc of rejection

(the lone edge of presence)

my mind is a coloured liquid
and very little more

the sweetbreads of inactivity,
how the pantleg softens with sloth,
and an overabundance of comfort
gnaws at the skin

I mark the zoology
of my unhappiness
and catalog it for an absent crowd

choked with self

this distended hour
chokes off speech
at the hilt

the freight of emotion
calves each moment off
into the next

my pain becomes a bath,
jelly green

a shaped scream.

there is peace in this pain,
in its constancy
filling every quarter

the scream is the marble
from which I carve these words

a memory dislodges into active
searing yellow
of the upper cavity

all is being
shook loose
and great tears fall
like tiles from the rooftops

I see with muscle
stretched taut
around the neck bone

there are no rules

uncertainty so pervasive negates
itself, becomes faith
in the disrobed dark

eyed up caverns of heat
loosen into atmosphere

we make a life of
second guesses, a shack
battened with brightly
coloured cereal boxes

this skulking cat

is need itself

my guts ringing
like a brass jug struck
with a mallet

TWO

anaesthetize the hideous gaps
the grey matter
the caravels of waste

aestheticize the feeble light
the way it can harm
and provoke exhaustion
in the occult maroon jelly
of your bones

make trinkets, gewgaws, bibelots, baubles,
from this clamorous mess
lest it engulf, then endorse
your corpse with all its hassled suggestion

anechoic solitude,
vacuum sealed in your despair,
done sous-vide

ice coruscates
on the sill

concoct the syllabary of your dejection

the rain divulges
air into the dotted eaves

there, a fragrance
to shroud me with

step into the rain
make an entrance

the first fine frost
tingeing the brick silver

collecting dawn, the apple,
folds up its redness

the telethon of our days—
whose line is it anyway?

there is a styrofoamness
to my low moments

I interact with packaging,
and this all can feel like an endless
unboxing

(show us the gaudy bauble!)
(enough of the bubblewrap!)

digest this waste.
maul it with my wrists,
allow the long degree
of its awakening

shrug the debris shroud

the grey plaster
between frames

when the blank of the interstice
asserts itself
and stitches one in

is when I spin out
into the fleck-riddled
float tank of boredom

shade over
with the pins of cowardice

the claws of purposelessness
silk harshly on the hardwood

having bamboozled myself
into another puff piece

I wince against the countertop

we're all just somebody

a catastrophe of meaning
without course
breaks upon the eyes
flawed white

I am catapulted into where I am
and the air concusses around me

to be between painting and easel,
to ease yourself
into inseam

as soon as we are conscious
we become parody

the razor scrapes
against the jawbone

we slip on the carcasses
of what we once said

I become horrible, then turn from it

the lascivious grit
tucked in a remote crick
of lowness

come to grips
hard at the table edge

minute black clumps
turn to looking at
a different winter

time, that cracked haberdasher
sews with teeth,
bedecks my back
with a sackcloth livery

I anaesthetize myself from pain
until pain becomes anaesthetic,
narcotic, carnal

the air breathes me in
full of fugue

a pulmonic tinge,
smoked glass

lopsided carriage
swivels on the roadkill

this soft calliper
is a vicious instrument, lodges
a tunnel of loss

I scrim here
the limits of this slump

an abscessual speech

birdstatic

I am rent and I
bleed beige

the world is rerendered
rear-ended

styrofoam, magazines, caulking

light of the deep end—

even your ankle
singes me
in the preamble to our parting

the pains and pleasures of context

pleasure pleasure pleasure

ugh

moses parted
the sea, I have trouble
parting my hair

these are just some things

the parts do not organize

terminal levity

ambushed
by a phalanx of tears
washing the crisper

the mundane is not sweet, it is heartbreaking,
the word heartbreaking
is heartbreakingly mundane.

big soft oranges, easy to peel

a vase:
vicious
viscous
viscera
vesicle
vas deferens
vascular
vesuvius
vasectomy

this bitter sherbet

drawing in a curtain of silt
I sidle up against
silken lowness

I needle you, unregenerate

smoking for the poses
the posy blooming red
tips the hot white cylinder

(we all fall down)

I, detritivore
let dissolve

dissolute afternoon after afternoon
swaying in the mangroves of despair

I eutrophicate

plangent in the wetlands

in the coves and inlets
lolling aimlessly

swishing from cyan to cerulean
grazed by the black kelp
of knowing

I am taunted all over
by modulation
breathing as coals
in the cooling pit

one moment I don't care a lick
and then am licked with care
its rough tongue, its sharp breath,
its slavering

I step into the bawling night
the melismatic dark
and its sequinned passing

I consume distraction itself
gorge on the flitting,
expand the blank between frames,

the blinks.

until it swallows, leaves me
a tangled fist
in my frontal lobe.

I fiddle the dire root.

the moon-covering cloud
a shoal of silver shade,
stitching through the spindrift

let that be a poem

stitched into the interstice

its nothing at all like what you see in the pictures

you left the door open
and a panther slinked through,
its dangerous calm

I am folded shaking
in the blue wicker my ankle
open the whole
bracing around me

a kind of embrace—
the town about man—

the eyeless fishes of luck
drift listless
across my retina

pilly with regret
in the abyssopelagic plateau

of days

the aftermath of whale fall
its light-dappled back
dyeing out into depth

the vaulted ribs stripped of flesh

by a passing murmur
of shimmering silver

gawp at the drifting bits
the shredded remnants
of this giant—

I, detritivore.

washed ashore, a common wreck
to find in nature
but a vessel for our moods

shunted along
this clanging track
one wishes almost
to choke it off

fishboning its throat
and leaving at least
a little glowing red
where one stuck

after some moments
the plummet goes still—
the ears stop popping
the water glass clatters to a halt

one adjusts.
one has lunch.
one checks one's messages,
one does a few dishes,
leaves some undone.

pain is indifference after all

coiled, the chaos charcoal
apoplectic stars

followed by the slug trail
of future regrets

this one sootless disk
catalects to bits before me
tobogganing into script

to feel the brows stone slab
sliding down, and dejection
sidling over beside me

this empty meridian
to which I cannot, but always,
return

these faint scratchings,
the blind beast
stalking overhead

longing's lacunae,
its edgeless lagoon
seeps up from the pink sand.

let me live in this longing,
in its greening I-beam,
it's sweet duress

pleasure's little snitch
its divergent smarting
the sordid bit

ambient diatribes
swell to a fuzz

follow the feed,
its blurred gunnels
rushing on
this cataract of slivers
pouring into
that endless basin

I swallow metallic,
pouring through moments

singe me a song, she says

THE SONG

*

*

*

*

FOUR

in the breadth of this impasse
I stultify

the bass, an ache
and higher up, a cleaving pang

and the clipped phrase again
bone in the hot broth
soaking up marrow

and the pelagic density
of the everyday,
this tide of things
rocking against the skull's
astonished coves

yes, yes

the breath's topography
is all that this world is,
just a symptom of breathing after
all

striking something but then
you slip off before you know
it, well, I'll
pivot then

into a different syntagm,
and jag violently from
this pathetic yawping
cawl, this string of civet
and out into

the slight difference of madness,
the grey edge
where the picture's slipped

I wash ashore
into awareness
changed into the same man
I was just moments before

the wind's patois
on this window,
among the clustered
brick habitations

the pelagic realm
the water column

"there is no place
for attachment, no
bottom for burrowing, nothing
to hide behind."

I am trying to dance myself
into someone else

momently buoyed
by a passing swathe
of oxidation

otherworlding

arrhythmic, the links clink

I am become
the valet of my own life,
it's ill-fitting bell-boy

things are embarking around me,
and yet here I lie, embargoed,
barged in algae

shame's pale velour
brushes the velum of my arm
as I pass
into an armistice of sorts

a lack of traction,
where slippage is the rule,
breakage the rule

you and I, comorbid in this room

this slow subsidence
the sand seeping down

in the dark we become all mouth—

starved, those shining lures
draw us in

"Imagine spending your life
floating weightless in
the air, never touching
the ground"

that darting clarity,
its rheum edge
upon the eyelid

and the air is humid with grief
palms sprouting from the dried salt

attention makes an atmosphere

2 eyes, 1 seeing
2 lungs, 1 breathing
etc.

sight swells worlds,
the egg in the belly of the snake

in the corners,
the mirror's smoked
burnishings

I have been banished out into
this marbling half-circle,
mobled in felt,
immobilized

I daze through life,
dazzled numb,
grazing on nervous crudités

I search for a good second, then
move on

that between thing, the spot
where the eye goes dim

pain and pleasure's clipping plateau
a gauze of sand
their endless mesa
ragged and pure
a place to rest on

draped over my skull
is the rest of me
a coat on its hook

curtailed, curtained in—
all is eggshell till it's touched

wondering beyond the
limits of this din, scrimming
it

the solid schlock
of the slot machine

the curtain of beeps

and blinks.

for a thin sustenance,
a drift of krill
filtering in the open throat

I feel at once
the endless depth behind my eyes

ungovernable itch
swoops in the vacant lots
of my scaffolding

a slow explosion of the senses
into one swelling sense

I jettison down the incorrigible
path

often almost careening off

the glancing of fists

one big smear campaign

pacific bliss

grief's rotunda,
its obsessional roundabout

above and below what can be heard,
here in the gutter

liquor swilled through teeth
grown thin with weeping

the air webbed with revenue
streams shot through
with barbed flies

the day became one long hour
like a busted lung,
wheezing into night

each second trying to shed itself
only to find its shell doubled,
soon sedimenting into stone

I tangle with the morass
only to sink deeper,
each lifted limb
leaves a hoarse sucking sound
in the epoxied air

heavied with dream

my surroundings sallow out
of meaning and into
blight

in the rain pocked
pothole of checking
messages

this careening off out into
the moment deforested

loose thoughts gather
in the damp moldings,
shattered saplings
scattered on the ice patch

tipping the ballast
and spinning off out into
this dimensionless presence,
this vagabond point

this is a coal-seam fire

nerves snapt
from all that wringing

a slug from the palm
full of heat

this is a spin-off,
a glossing
over

the image sinking,
sunk in

the canted frame framed
with endless nothing

awash with TV
Reality, faces
bisected by their own becoming

and trailing off again out into

bag tree, shouldered by wind,
dearth web, sundered below
the flat split of cloud

and this crack-walled plot
with its withered crop

soldering thoughts together,
smouldering reek of lead

the plumbing visible,
this kitchen-sink martyrdom

I, detritivore

pointless, stale martyrdom

falling through time,
your voice rains through

FIVE

habit is an atmosphere
the unraveling tapestry
the juddering edge
juddering

the close zebras of the outer eye
and the everything
I

ignore it
the spinning spigot
sternum lodged
and all this
spinning-jenny's unspooling

pooling where I am

as breath can pool
like oil

the particulate grip
of emergency,
the hastening of insides out
the spackled lung hacking,
its lurid bloom, its neon
accretions

reality is that
towards which the wave
rushes, brushes then
scatters in retreat

I am scattered in retreat

hello?

and always it is sweeter
on the other side of something
the air sweeter
the light lighter

windows
hovering
in windows:
a way out
without a way

a thought-world of sphagnum moss
ever on the edge
of ignition

a thought-world
of sphagnum moss, ever on
the fluttering edge of ignition

rolling forth
like tears, frothing
like a wave, the seconds
hasten, fasten me
here fascination spun
in liquid silk
of sheol serpent shorn

the urge to write
"bitumen": bitumen

winter-thewed,
wind-muscled

the fervid scroll,
its long scrape
with death

upon which wind draft
am I perched,
hammocked in
what low-slung cause?

silence (death's chauffeur)

a hoarse thrum of notes emanates
from the mottled brass curve

noise (life's embalming fluid)

this habitual landscape
of caulking and bitumen

announced in the annealing,
what empty signs
sink from the rising
smoke?

this is ghost fishing

I wash myself of night
skein of dream
pulled drainward

my head hums
with the garbage truck
and headlights sliding
over the far green wall

experience is a room
we carry with us,
as the snail does its shell and sometimes

I wish for a demolition artist
to blow mine up
and allow me that brief encasement
of undiluted light

instead of this one
rounded carapace
and its carousel of phantoms

its liquid shadow and solar flare
its dim bulb spinning in the unchecked dark
the cellar in which hope's
sordid morsels are stored

the wall diamond-cast
with another car's passing

and always some corner
of garment catches in brushing

the brambles of
bewilderment, leaving
a loop of thread
just wide enough
to glimpse the world thru
and thru

mostly, the world
is texture

this room, the quiet black
insides of a fiddle
upon which no one
is fiddling

and yet still it reverberates
with the shadows of far off foot fall,
muffled, a flicker
of fading golden sound
and sanity swaying
on its pedicel

the cockles of distraction
hushing on the shore,
that rasping maraca

the fruits are ransomed,
hanging silent & beyond
reach before me

to whose tribute
should I this seeking
river pay?

the fog of enjoyment, the yellow
fog, receipts, pennies, a sour
candy, free with every goodbye

snow's million interruptions
wall all around
and all falls with it

surrounded in sound,
shrouded, swaddled,
clouded, crowded out by it

vermillion interruptions
when the blood's blank
asserts itself, inserts
itself into this endless
non-conversation
of ours, of days, of years

I circulate this black lake
on my cracked plastic pedalo

the clock strokes the hour
the minute the second the
deci the centi the
milli micro nano pico
bento atto zepto
yocto planck breaks
and I drop
down and

down

SIX

slumped in the couch
shouldered into poetry

attention leaps at times
a silver fish
caught in a brief brake
of light through the cloud cover,
cold clover blooms

the fabric of my seeing loosens
into a swirling hypnosis of sound

I rootbeer float through life

the lung is spreading,
lungeing into the new

the air radiant with particles

the branches shiver with what they bring forth
what violent life they froth with

crosses to dot the landscape

matter's secret writhing burst

an actor's cough upon the real air

bustle ignites a rustling breath,
sighs gone rust-wrought
(a fatal announcement)

I speak languish

this black net cast
across us all

united under this novel god

roped into a prayerful
gasping

breath's veil shadowed
by another breathing

industry's wheeze
heard in the gutters
ringing through the pipes

with cloud finger bent, beckoned
to bring forth either music or
infection

this our slow subsumption
our sumped summing up
begins, becalmed
by that thought

by the fire's blossom,
the bulbs flashing into flower
on the still cold branch

lungs collapse
like markets

clumps of ash,
wet with rain,
after the airstrike

revelation revealing
revelation alone,
stripping back
the stripping back

this waving monody,
this string silvering over

a luxurious itch
rankles the body's biota

twinned-stars
whirlpooling the waters,
the whippoorwill pinned
to its song

a becoming to terms

vision but an outer eyelid,
a sail swollen
with starry wind

the air moiréd
with the eye's twitching

the leaves wave, the waves
leave, the grasses, the
bushes all ashiver, the

past and future interleaved
like hands in prayer, hold me
here

the world provides
new metaphors for the body

blood in tremolo
rib cage trilling

meaning a strain
on this glassed breath,
a satin gloss or
blemish in the bone white
jade, rottening the tusk

we dawn the bloodhood

my pulse clicks faintly
in the early morning hours, ears
ringing faintly

this bright net cast,
shining spirit surges, laces
through the populace
stowed in the nicks and gullies
of our daily merchandises
in the lines and divots
of merchant's palm
luggaged in the substance

the heart of the deal

over every shook hand, death
stands its thin attendance

mother stews rhubarb &
chrysanthemum for the coming months

identity a kind of illness
impressed upon the living flesh

the smile dissolves
upon the face, the face
of the water dissolves
the sky's white mantle

within the moving face
a black stillness
a dark pivot upon which
expression revolves

the breath a boat
rocking on the belly's edge

and words like forcing a ball under
water

as vision is eyelash tinged
is the world tinged
with another world's wind, another wind's world

a tide which swoops and drags

us into the next
now the trees
bristle with warm growing
goosebumps as we speak

no change, only a surface inswell
and some who in somnolence
dip into sleep, and come up
cups abrim

the bowl of sound
chirped in spots
glints with ore
and mica rock

the same rain
stitches through

remain in
remain in
remain in

smokes from the pathways
in new spring heat

the quiet of death comforts now
the quiet of carrion
carried skyward

the scabbard slipt, the picked scab

the taut unending wound

the myelin sheath
the violin case
black velvet lined

it rolls back the eyes

this the zero-aura of our days

seashells scatter the mountaintops—
slow snow

terrible rightness

remain in

now unbraced with thought
I collapse into plateau
then apse up with water

vision hums with vision
the clouds come screeching by

as light as light
playing on the grasses

I look for a mood with room
to unbraid me
from this method of breathing
and into total contact,
enact a concentration

but I sallow in place
fidgeting into
a definitive spinning out
all infinitives split
with a thin hissing sound

the home ticks

dissimulating on
the second's liquid adze

I look down at ape's feet
clothing the floor

the eyelid blooms
with brief tattoos

the dark blooms

I idle around
limpid in the lamplight
make corners where I settle
where I sidle up next to

hovels of slovenliness
backstroke through lukewarm
pools of penumbra

the punctured kiddy pool
of my afternoon

velveted with grease
and trickles into evening

the problem of one's own mind

the hours melt, the days melt

low below, the willows
sweep dew from the grasses

and those hollow sockets of doom

the self is itself in retreat,
fingertipping the impossible

the wind draws the flowers
in, panging towards the sky
their stems solid with agony
& petals shiver with guilt

the guilty flowers
bury their heads in the wet
black soil

the unfelt rain
calls the mind
to begin its unlacing

your gut once more
a bowl of becoming
a pitcher of bilious flowers

an outcrop of mushrooming
nibbled by the wild
mare as it gazes
off into the black moulting
starriness of a threshold

the word's threshold

this belch-pocked speech
makes a space in which the self
may slither

what silent musics
mould our moods

what slidden tuning
draws us through
time's fucked up glissandi

and into slow dissolution
and plastic agony

faint rumours have gathered
in the fruiting bulbs
trees murmur
this is afterlife

limbs loosen by cricks
by death-painless degrees

stare out from the dark
am stared on the spot spotless

marbled with perception
septic with sitting
all is felted over with feeling

and fuzzy from the lush life

from the glimpses, the discards
the endless trash of things
I surmise a negative topography

cut glass blue
like water knowing
its first light

the hum like electronics,
like speakers between music

awareness hollows all it touches,
tunnels through the body

(the blurst of times)

blustering through the reticule
the keys slipt thru a rip in the silk
his frenzy grows slender branches
spindle down his throat
and tickles him dizzy

we are after all but an organ purse,
as his mother would say

spurned into liquidation
everything must go

guffawing into sumpland
he coughs mesozoically

the computer fans hum
into the backseat velour
of childhood illnesses

the same mottled cosmos

I remember the car forest green

the same crushed grey plush
upon which I sat
and threw up on

the texture of distances
the faint residue of travel
one forgets to shower off

and the tree a reservoir
of shadow still

brightness hisses then
crackles into gaps,
expands into ocean foam

chatter grows along the skull's
curve like molecules diagramming
into honeycomb, and here

pours the sweet honey
wings crunch
like spun sugar,
like wintered spindrift

dissimulates into product

wallowed in white
waylaid in wool
woven warm

putting fist to brow
fizzes like soda
into a pretend concentration,
dilutes thought with air

how to sum it,
this landscape

engorged by various vessels
we tremulate into endless
states of effulgence

heresiarchs of movement
airborne again and again and again
then not is to feel landlocked

habitual modes crowbarred,
lines of attack scrambled
in the skillet of new-knowing

and loneliness a streak of fat
shrieking, shrinking into grease
the body but a severed wave,
waves & flaps disgustingly,
weights into the bed
ditches into sleep
tossing dirt with every shallow
breath turning soil
into flowerings

and the day warped with beigeouts

does the world scream at the eye,
or does the eye scream the world at us?

(the archbishopric of malady)

(sleazing into paranoia)

(how now to lick shut the envelope)

look how the monkeys scream from the trees,
their eyes jaundiced

the harmonies of disaster
thaw and hatch along the glass's edge

at the crest of the breath, briefly
a death

I look to my fartherland

the bear ragged stalks
thin, claws at fish
among the waning floes
the shining sheeted distance
shook as foley thunder
a sheering tundra light
splays the blind shadow
across the whitewash

page so bright it stains the eye

the dew undone by noon

sound the debts
the spine of guilt

the gorgeous greys
the blanketing all

he speaks like the rain
on and on

stuck in this elevator shaft

the cat stalks past,
muffles the rain

wild towers bristle with dawn

the wave speaks vaguely
of the rocks beneath

a world of constant
interruption irrupts
non-stop before us
our fascination suction cupping
us to it, flattened out
into a shining parallel
a faceless moment
depthless reflection
tremor without cause

bone white roots writhing in the black soil
milking for its meat

distraction refreshes
into traction
and then the sweet sliding off

she checks her black pixels
in the sheen of the limo door

those deciduous moments

this brackish pleurality

history hacks away at us

in noonday's copse
the noon rots

my flesh a rich loam
fit for rifling through
primed for supping

we organize now
into one collapsing lung
one soot choked plurality
that morbid tickle is time
spreading its one grey wing
taut as drumskin
your life writ in vein

when wonder winnows,
maundering through shallow waters
ambershot
caught in weed tangle

lashes the light, lashed
to the world low lidded,
then unleashed into
lifelessness

every leaf a swinging gate
death life, life death, etc.

fed on hunger, the stomach's own
becoming a gnawing kind of
nourishment, welcomes in worlds

and all moods pierced
on one pin, centred on
one endless plunging down

turns into up
ended into endless and all
shadows quenched of themselves

for many a beam reached
but left splinter shod
these my splinters
displayed before ye

sweet duress, all call
for envelopment
as the body envelops its insides

each crevice embellished
with sun or another such substance

a tenantable restlessness this

life passes through us
as shadows over grain
black shadows over golden grain
black cloud shadows over golden fields of the grain

this is the end
of the world. no, this
is the end of
the world. no, this is
the end of the
world. no, this is the
end of the world.
no,

ACKNOWLEDGMENTS

Thanks to *Touch the Donkey*, where parts of this book appeared.

Thanks to my mother Rebecca, my father Michael, and my step-father Cary for always encouraging me not just in my poetry, but in all my creative pursuits.

Thanks to my sister Elena for being an early reader of this book and a constant support.

Thanks to Richard Greene, who was my supervisor in university while I wrote this book, and helped give me the confidence to walk down a new and uncertain path.

Thanks to Chris Loose, who gave me invaluable feedback as I wrote this book during our meetings when we would workshop each other's poems.

Thanks to Carmine Starnino, for taking on this strange manuscript from an unknown poet.

And thank you to all the friends and teachers, past and present, known and unknown, who opened my eyes to the wonders of language.

NOTE

The language in this book comes from all over. Within you'll find quotations from biology textbooks, snippets of overheard early spring conversations, fragments of subway ads, lines from the Simpsons, the din of the newsfeed, Emily Dickinson, Planet Earth. I tried to use the refuse, to refuse nothing, to let it all in. I honestly forget where most of it comes from, but I think my poetry comes out of forgetting, the way we're soon forgotten in the loaming, only to bloom again.

Talya Rubin • Richard Sanger • Stephen Scobie
Peter Dale Scott • Deena Kara Shaffer
Carmine Starnino • Andrew Steinmetz • David Solway
Ricardo Sternberg • Shannon Stewart
Philip Stratford, trans. • Matthew Sweeney
Harry Thurston • Rhea Tregebov • Peter Van Toorn
Patrick Warner • Derek Webster • Anne Wilkinson
Donald Winkler, trans. • Shoshanna Wingate
Christopher Wiseman • Catriona Wright
Terence Young